# LESSONS
## *from the*
# LONG RUN

*JAY McCHORD*

*Contact the author at jaymcchord@gmail.com*

Printed in the United States of America
ISBN  978-0-9827519-6-1

Cover Design by Robert Bridges
Interior Design by Rhonda Dragomir

PAVILION BOOKS
PO Box 8653
Lexington, KY  40533

Visit our website at www.pavilionbooks.com

*Pavilion* books

# Endorsements

For decades, Jay McChord has been a catalyst for innovation and transformation …*Lessons* is a powerful, yet practical, tool for personal transformation and creating new horizons for the reader.

### Matt O'Neil
*Senior Pastor, Watershed Church / Marathon Runner*

Jay has the unique ability to make everyone in the room believe anything is possible and this book will motivate you to go far beyond where you are today!

### Michele DeJesus, PhD
*Fitness & Nutrition Specialist/ Marathon Runner*

Through this book my friend Jay makes us all aware we all need others in our life to not only finish our journey, but do it in a joyous and rewarding way.

### Doug Flynn
*Former MLB player (2-time World Series Champion/Gold Glove Winner)*

After training and racing with Jay for years I have been the beneficiary of the insights of this book. It is packed with motivation for runners and non-runners alike.

### Brennan Donahoe
*2-time Ironman Finisher*

*LESSONS* IS A MUST READ for everyone. It helped me achieve a life-long dream, finishing a full marathon. Jay's practical coaching and spiritual insights will lead to great success in your Long Run of Life.

**MILES PHELPS**
*Founder, By the Spirit Ministries and Marathon Runner*

THIS IS NOT JUST ANOTHER self- help book. Jay has masterfully written wisdom and inspiration for our body, soul and mind.

**ERNIE PERRY**
*Senior Pastor, Broadway Christian Church*

JAY McCHORD LOOKED ME IN THE EYES over lunch one day and captured another one of his PR's ("Persons Recruited"). As an overweight, unhealthy man approaching his 40's, I would have never laced up the shoes without Jay's encouragement. Within six months I completed a 5k, 10k, and a 15k. Jay's "Lessons from the Long Run" will encourage you greatly on this journey we all share.

**ERIC GEARY**
*President, Lexington Leadership Foundation*

AS AN AVID RUNNER and workout enthusiast, *Lessons From the Long Run* rekindled my passion for training and running. But as a follower of God, I quickly discovered the parallels of running the race of life as the Scriptures leapt off the page and embedded in my heart. Jay speaks with devout truth, both from experiences of running and also from life lessons he has encountered publically, privately, professionally, politically and personally. This book will challenge you and inspire you to never give up!

**DOUG PIATT**
*Executive Minister, Broadway Christian Church/ Marathon Runner*

THIS BOOK OFFERS a level of awareness about life I could not verbalize. This book is for runners and never-will-be runners alike.

**ANNETTE MANLIEF**
*Wife, Mom and Marathon Runner*

# ACKNOWLEDGMENTS

As this book will point out, we cannot run the *Long Run* alone. We need to continually draw strength and support from others if we are to finish our race well. There are those who run alongside us every step of the way and others who cheer us on and encourage us from the sidelines (in racing vernacular they are called our "Curb Crew"). Regardless whether they are someone who bears the burden of our every step or they are simply the one who cheers and encourages at key points along the way, the fact remains we need to pause and acknowledge those who made it possible to *run* our race. Here are mine...

Thank you first and foremost to God, who created me, gave me abilities and talents, strengths and weaknesses, a course to run and true companionship throughout my (ongoing) race.

Thank you to my wife( and *Homecoming Queen*), Jennifer. Without your pushing and encouragement to finish this project it would still be a jumble of notes that "someday might make a good book." You make a fantastic running partner in the race of life and I love you very much!

Thank you to Riley and Davis. It is because of you two that I am forever 19 (in my mind)!

Thank you to my entire family (especially Mom, Dad and Candy) for always supporting me (even when you had no clue what I was talking about).

Thank you to Jeremy & Barbara Brewer who conned...I mean, *convinced* me to run that first marathon in 2002 and started this entire line of thinking. Thank you also to Matt O'Neil, Miles & Melanie Phelps, Eric Geary, Warren & Carol Rogers, Todd & Amanda Bledsoe, Phil & Marnie Holoubek, Kevin Stinnett, George Myers, Jim & Mollie Sawyer, Donna & Cecil Williams, Ernie & Pam Perry, Doug Piatt, Flo Morguelan, Joey Pickett, Earl Ogata, Joshua Collins, Tom Evans, Mo Lloyd, Evan and Jackie Watson, Mike Lesshafft, Brennan Donahoe & Annette Manlief, Mary Beth Nauman & Kevin Compton, Clay Coburn, Brewster McLeod, Chris Wells, Eric Bumm, Dr. Michele DeJesus & Paul Schmuck (my "Life Coach"), Scott Brewer, T. Lynn Williamson, Larry True, Jack & Kathy Kelly, Diana Doggett, Mark & Lina Brewer, David Whitehouse, Nathan & Mary Richie, Brent Claiborne, Jeff Fox, JD & Ali Denton, John Barnette, Ross Barnette, Joe Lane, Doug Flynn (#23), Stephanie Clarke, William Green, Chris McCoy, Morgan Chapman, Miles Meehan, Jon Weece, Rusty George, TD Oaks, Monte Wilkinson, Woody Church, Bob & Connie Pitman, Jim &Jan O'Kelley, Phil & Nancy Boatman (the ultimate matchmakers), Rick & Nancy Pounds, Vitale Buford, Paula Schrecker and Gerald Belcher.

Yes, there are quite a few names on this list but each one of these folks has had a profound impact on my life and needs to be acknowledged (publically) as being a difference-maker in my life.These people have helped me, taught me, encouraged me, fed me, supported me, challenged me, affirmed me and in some cases even confronted me. Each one is a contributor to this book and I wanted them (and you the reader) to know how important they are to me!

Thank You All!

Jay Mc

# How to
# Use This Book

While simple and easy to read, this book is designed to challenge your thinking and actions. To fully receive all this book has to offer consider the following:

- Read/ work through this book with a family member or friend(s).

- Give ample time to spend on each chapter. No need to rush through.

- Spend time considering the Question and Challenge offered at the end to each "Mile" (Chapter). Use the space provided (use extra space if needed) to write down your responses to those Questions and Challenges.

- Use the blank "Worksheet" pages in the back to write down the lessons you have learned from your long run.

- Share your lessons with others…AND WITH US. Submit your lessons for potential future publications to:

**www.lessonsfromthelongrun.com**

# TABLE OF CONTENTS

# WARM UP

## IT'S ALL ABOUT THE STRETCHING AND BEING STRETCHED

*God says, "My thoughts are higher than your thoughts"*
*Isaiah 55:8*

STRETCHING IS VITAL to any pre-race activity. I began to see that word, *stretching*, in a different light recently. There is something about the act of being stretched that is vital to the *Race of Life*.

Stretching can also be defined as the act of thinking bigger thoughts, traversing distances never imagined and/or expanding threshold for pain and endurance.

I remember training for my first marathon and thinking, "You know this race kills people…heck the first guy that attempted this distance at the Battle of Marathon DID die! What in the world is going to happen to me?" Obviously I didn't die (to the contrary, I caught the long distance bug in a big way!) but I did find myself constantly being "stretched" in that process as I spent 18 weeks mentally and physically preparing to go further and endure more than I ever had before.

That exercise of *Thinking Bigger* and *Being More* than we once imagined is what this book is designed to do for you.

This simple book is constructed in the format of a marathon (26.2 Chapters to represent 26.2 miles of that race). Each chapter pairs a running concept with scripture to give you something *Bigger* to think about.

The scripture verses are purposely offered in fragmented (sometimes, paraphrased) form because that is how they would come to me while running. As you work through this book I would challenge you to look up the actual verse and consider what it says in its full context.

Each chapter then concludes with a specific Question and Challenge (along with space to journal what you will do) so that this little book may serve as a catalyst for changing your life.

Hope you enjoy the journey!

# The Power of a Partner

*"Two are better than one...and a cord of three strands is not easily broken."*
*Ecclesiastes 4:9, 12*

IT HAS BEEN MY EXPERIENCE that only a rare few are able to train properly and complete a long race like the marathon totally by themselves. On the other hand, I have seen over and over (and especially with my own personal running experience) that the single most important factor to successfully completing a race is to have someone who will "do it with you."

When you look at your training schedule and it calls for an obscene distance to run that day ("obscene" is defined differently by each one of us, but YOU KNOW what that term means when you see it ☺), it is so much more bearable if you know someone is coming out with you to do it. While the accountability factor comes into play, I contend the "comrade factor" may be more important.

Knowing that someone else is "walking (running, in this case) a mile in your shoes" goes a very long way in getting you through the tough stuff.

**QUESTION:** Who is "with you" in your life right now? Who is running with you consistently and understands the challenge(s) you face? Who is someone that encourages you to do the tough stuff because they are as well?

**CHALLENGE:** Identify those who you want to run with you. Encourage them to do this "race" together. Meet consistently. Hold each other accountable. Realize what it says that "two are better than one."

God

Stacy

Megan

_____

_____

_____

_____

_____

_____

_____

_____

_____

_____

_____

_____

_____

_____

_____

_____

_____

_____

_____

# WHY?

*"...for fear that all my efforts had been wasted and
I was running the race for nothing."*
*Galatians 2:2*

WHY ARE YOU RUNNING?

So often I hear people say, "I want to run a marathon." My question to them is, "Okay...so why are you going to run it?" Is it a Bucket list item? Is it because you are looking for a new challenge? Maybe it's because you reached a certain age? Or maybe is it to raise awareness and money for a cause that has your heart?

One of the most important questions to wrestle with is, "Why are you running the race you are in?" Because training for long runs can be such a grind and so painful it really does help if you know why you are running.

When you cross the finish line, the fulfillment is also so much greater if you have a specific reason for why you trained and ultimately succeeded in traversing that distance. In life it is also so much more gratifying to know why you are running the race. Why do you get out of bed every day and do the mundane (and sometimes painful) tasks necessary to succeed in this race called life?

The greatest tragedy in life is to come to the end and realize you "ran your race for nothing!"

**QUESTION:** Why are you running your race? For what purpose are you doing what you do every day? Why is this race meaningful/important to you?

**CHALLENGE:** Write down the specific reason(s) why you are running your race. What greater reason(s) do you want to have for running and finishing well? Articulate the importance of running your race with a purpose and a meaning…and then begin to tell people!

To have a better life for Megan Stacy and me

It is important to me to be clean live a Godly life and provide

# RUN **YOUR** RACE

*"Run the race that is marked out for you."*
*Hebrews 12:1*

THERE IS NOTHING WORSE than running someone else's race. What I mean is most runners have found themselves in the frustrating and painful place of running a race at the wrong pace.

A COUPLE EXAMPLES:

*Too Fast...*

When I was 15 years old I got swept up in the excitement of pacing with some elite runners in a 5k and did the first mile under six minutes. Needless to say, my wheels fell off shortly after that first mile and I ended up walking over half the race. I felt terrible and was so aggravated by my horrendous overall time that was solely due to getting caught up running someone else's race.

*Too Slow...*

A few years ago I was helping some friends train and complete their first Half Marathon. Both of them were beginners and never dreamed they could run that distance. To their credit they did all the training.

It was my commitment to run with one of these friends the entire way to make sure she crossed the finish line successfully. About seven miles into the 13.1 distance, my friend began to slow down considerably. My job was to keep pushing so she would not quit. We ultimately finished the race, but I was in severe pain due to slowing down (to the point of even running in place at times). That was someone else's pace, and by running at that pace, I was almost injured because I had taken too many steps.

*Too Far...*

I have a friend who (at the time of this writing) is attempting to run across America and whose route will allow him to touch every state on the way. His "race" has him running 14-19 miles, twice a day; 6 days a week (refer to Mile 7 Chapter on Resting). That is HIS race, not mine.

QUESTION: What is YOUR race pace? How fast/ slow do you need to go to "run your race" and cross the finish line successful (and uninjured)? Are others causing you to run their race? Who can push you, yet accompany you?

CHALLENGE: "Run YOUR race." Find the right pace and distance and don't watch anyone else. Write below what type of activity that looks like for you.

---

---

---

---

---

---

---

MILE

3

11

_____

_____

_____

_____

_____

_____

_____

_____

_____

_____

_____

_____

_____

_____

_____

_____

_____

_____

_____

# WHAT IS YOUR CAPACITY...REALLY?

*"If you have raced with men on foot and they have worn*
*you out, how can you compete with horses?"*
*Jeremiah 12:5*

HOW MANY TIMES DO YOU SEE people who tire doing something small...or nothing at all? How often do you see someone who has untapped potential but never realizes it, because they grow tired and decide to quit?

We each have so much more endurance than we can imagine. We read stories all the time of men and women who preserve in inconceivably difficult circumstances and think, "could I have done that?" As it relates to running, we all have looked at a long race and thought, "could I do that?"

Funny (but true) story:

A few years ago the winner of a marquee marathon was being interviewed about his record finish time of just over two hours. During the interview, he said with tremendous respect and admiration, "I am amazed that some people can run this race in five or six hours! I can't imagine running for that long."

So here is a man that many marvel at his capacity to cover 26.2 miles in just over two hours and he is equally astonished at other people who can pound pavement for five to six hours. Each party recognizes that there is so much more that is possible than what they have experienced.

**QUESTION:** Do you grow tired in the small things? If you knew you could not fail, what would you attempt?

**CHALLENGE:** Write down everything you would do if you knew you could not fail in doing it. Pick one thing on that list today and start working towards it. Push past your current position today and go further, faster and with greater endurance toward those things on that list!

_____

_____

_____

_____

_____

_____

_____

_____

_____

_____

MILE
4

15

# SEEING YOUR WAY

THERE IS A RACE IN KENTUCKY called "The Bourbon Chase." It is a 200-mile team relay race that requires each member of the 12person relay team to run three separate times over the course of about 26-30 hours (depending on how fast your team is). One of the unique aspects of this particular race is that at least one of your legs is run in complete darkness.

The race itself winds through some of the most amazing rural countryside you can imagine, BUT...that countryside is lost in complete pitch black darkness when your leg is at four a.m.

Another aspect of this race is there are only 200 teams involved. For much of your time on the course you never interact with another runner. Thus, even though each runner is required to wear a headlamp, those pitch black/middle of the night legs are exceedingly lonely and very dark.

*It was during my 8.7 mile leg at 4 a.m. that this chapter was developed.*

As I was running down a lonely, dark, two lane road with no one around and with just the light on my cap, I realized even though that little light was very small, it still allowed me to see what was right in front of me. It was a "lamp unto my feet and a light unto my path."

Sometimes we say we want to see what the future holds (i.e. the road marked out in front of us). Sometimes there are times in life where we actually get to see that path clearly. But there are many more times in life where we can only see the next step in front of us.

What was so clear on that dark night was, as long as "this little light of mine" was pointed straight in front of me I could see exactly where to go. When I moved my head and became distracted, I had a greater chance of stumbling, getting hurt and/or not finishing the race that was marked out for me.

Having that light, even if it was very small, was a guide that allowed me to get where I needed to go.

**QUESTION:** When life is all darkness around you and it is impossible to see the big picture and the length of the road ahead do you find yourself looking side to side in distraction or even stopping?

**CHALLENGE:** Today, consider forgetting about all that big stuff with all its potential distractions and just simply laser focus your attention on putting the next foot in front of the other. Point your light where it needs to be, take the next step and then repeat (frequently)! Write down what the exact next step(s) need to be for you.

_____

_____

_____

_____

_____

# PAIN OF DISCIPLINE VS. PAIN OF REGRET

*"All athletes are disciplined in their training.*
*They do it to win a prize..."*
*I Corinthians 9:25*

I ONCE HEARD A MAN SAY, "There are only two types of pain in the world, the pain of discipline and the pain of regret. The pain of discipline weighs ounces but the pain of regret weighs tons!"

The verse above speaks directly to this man's statement. "ALL athletes seeking to win a prize" deal with the pain of discipline; the pain of early morning workouts, running the long miles, eating right, getting enough sleep, pushing muscles and lungs further and on and on.

If they do not deal with (and experience) the pain of discipline they will have to contend with the pain of regret! Regret of knowing that IF they had only gotten up on those mornings, run the long miles, eaten right, slept correctly and pushed their bodies hard, they could have attained the prize they pursued.

It is so easy to stay in bed on cold or nasty weather days. It is easy to cut distances short because of fatigue (perceived or real). It is easy to eat unhealthy food, to stay up late watching TV and certainly to not push your body past where it feels comfortable. To achieve the goal you aspire to, you must instill discipline to counteract all of the "easy and comfortable" decisions. Discipline offers a certain degree of pain. But as the man said, "the pain of discipline weighs ounces but the pain of regret weighs tons!"

**QUESTION:** What "prize" are you working toward? What areas of your life require discipline to reach that prize? What is the pain associated with the discipline in that area (or to those areas)? If you do not apply discipline, what types of regret may you eventually or ultimately experience?

**CHALLENGE:** Using the space below or a separate sheet of paper, write out detailed answers to the questions above. After finishing that exercise, highlight the words (sentences) describing the pain you will experience with <u>Discipline</u>. Then highlight the words (sentences) describing the pain you will experience with the <u>Regret</u>. Put each highlighted word (or sentence) under the appropriate heading of "Ounces" or "Tons." Look at that sheet to daily as a reminder to do the things necessary to live with no regret!

_____

_____

_____

_____

_____

_____

_____

_____

_____

MILE
6

# REST

*"...so on the 7th day God rested from all His work"*
*Genesis 2:2*

---

IF GOD THOUGHT IT IMPORTANT ENOUGH to rest one day a week from His labor of creation do you think it might be wise to do the same? In our rush-around/ get-it-done-yesterday world we seldom see any value in resting. Rest, in fact, is viewed oftentimes as a nice word for laziness. The opposite is actually true.

Our bodies are built to handle amazing stresses and strains. They have unbelievable capacities that are hard to even fathom. The problem is we run these tremendous machines so hard for so long that we cause them to break down.

At some point in a runner's experience they come face to face with "over-training." Simply put, they do not build specific times to rest into their training. They (we) don't give our body a day each week to recover and heal.

When we do not allow for a consistent and planned [weekly] time of rest (a day where there is no mileage or heavy physical exertion) then our body decides to take its own break. Unfortunately, those breaks are generally painful, prolonged and untimely. There was an old advertising campaign slogan for cars that said, "You can pay me now or you can pay me later" that holds true for our bodies.

QUESTION: Do you take a day off each week from your "labor?" Do you consistently schedule time to be quiet and to rest the physical (and mental) exertion on your body? Are you running your body (and brain) too hard?

CHALLENGE: Take out your calendar and schedule 4 days of rest over the next 4 weeks. Plan for rest to be a part of your routine! In the space below write down (specifically) what resting looks like for you on those days. What specific activities allow you to rest, recover and recharge?

_____

_____

_____

_____

_____

_____

_____

_____

_____

_____

_____

27

# OH HOW EASY IT WOULD BE

*"I will be proud that I did not run the race in vain
and that my work was not useless."*
***Philippians 2:16***

AS A MARATHON GRINDS ON, you begin to hurt in places you did not know you could hurt. You are battling physical pain certainly, but at a marathon's later stages there is more mental pain to contend with. Your brain starts suggesting things like, "all this isn't worth it," "you are in too much pain to keep going," "people will completely understand if you can't continue."

While it is critical to listen to your body and to know if you are in trouble and are in need of medical assistance, it is also critical for you to know that the easiest thing to do sometimes is quit...especially if there is a warm and inviting place encouraging you to do so.

I know from my own experience that the "Drop Out" tent (these are medical tents with trained staff that are supplied with food, water, ice, and medicine for runners who just can't go any further) at Mile 20 or 21 of the 2007 Chicago Marathon almost enticed me to quit.

That race was a disaster in that the race field had been expanded to 45,000 runners that year, the weather was unseasonably hot for October, and the race coordinators did not supply enough water.

Those factors led to a perfect storm that saw hundreds sent to the ER and one man to lose his life. After witnessing the race degenerate into chaos, the race officials were forced to "call the race" and we were told to, "stop running because the race would not count."

Ha! Try telling THAT to thousands of people who trained for months (or years), who were already hours into this race! Even though my time would not "officially" count and I had been cramping for more than 10 miles, many of us kept moving forward to the Finish Line ...right past those very tempting Drop Out stations (with their beds, pillows and cold water!).

The 2007 Chicago Marathon started with 45,000 people, but less than half that number would run, walk or crawl across the Finish Line on that miserably hot day...I was among them! My race was not in vain!

**QUESTION:** Can you think of anything more futile (or "in vain") than training for months, putting in countless hours of work only to decide during the middle of the race to just quit? What temptations are you dealing with to quit running in this important race called life?

**CHALLENGE:** Write down every negative word you have heard that even remotely has tempted you to drop out or quit on your race. Take that list and, one at a time, declare them each a lie! Audibly hear yourself say, "I choose not to believe that because it is a lie and I am choosing instead to keep moving forward!"

_____

_____

_____

MILE

8

31

_____

_____

_____

_____

_____

_____

_____

_____

_____

_____

_____

_____

_____

_____

_____

_____

_____

_____

_____

MILE
9

# THE ROAR OF
# THE CROWD

*"Therefore, since we are surrounded by such a*
*huge crowd of witnesses..."*
*Hebrews 12:1*

IN 2002, I RAN MY FIRST MARATHON, the Chicago Marathon. One thing about this marathon is there a million people that line the 26.2 mile course and cheer everyone on to the finish. You are never left alone to run on any portion of the race.

There are places on that course, because there are so many people cheering, they actually spill off the curbs and press into the street around you. If your name is visible on your shirt they will call out your name and say things like, "Go Jay Go"…"You can do this"…"Looking great Jay"…"Keep it up, you are almost there"…"Run like you stole it Jay!"(That last one is absolutely my favorite and it never gets old).

It was on mile 10 of that race in 2002 that I thought about this verse from Hebrews. That verse describes being, "surrounded by such a great crowd of witnesses, cheering us on" and here I was literally being cheered on by a huge crowd of witnesses.

As the race progressed and the mileage stacked up, I thought about how hard it was to run 20 miles alone back in my hometown verses how "easy" (is 20+ miles ever really easy?) it was to run these miles with so many people encouraging me.

When we know that others are surrounding us to encourage and cheer us on, it lightens our loads and allows us to go further, faster and with greater endurance than we ever dreamed.

**QUESTION:** If you could see and hear millions of people around cheering you on today how much easy would your race be?

**CHALLENGE:** Picture millions of people lining a street you are running down (packed in shoulder to shoulder) all cheering you on to run well and finish strong. Hear them yelling, "Go (Your Name)! You can do it! Keep running! You are doing great! Whoooo Hoooo...look at you go! Looking good!"

Given that kind of cheering and support list out what would change in your outlook and how you would approach the challenges of today, this week or this year?

_____

_____

_____

_____

_____

_____

_____

_____

_____

# It Will Demand Endurance

*"And let us run with endurance, the race*
*God has set before us."*
**Hebrews 12:1**

WEBSTER'S DEFINES the word en•dur•ance as:

1.  the fact or power of **enduring** or bearing pain, hardships, etc.

2.  the ability or strength to continue or last, especially despite fatigue, **stress**, or other adverse conditions; stamina: *He has amazing physical endurance.*

3.  lasting quality; duration: *His friendships have little endurance.*

4.  something endured, as a hardship; trial.

It is a word most think of in the context of something done over a prolonged period that generally involves pain. This is an apt description of running a marathon! It is a long distance that is not over quickly and will extract pain from you. Heck, the amount of time, distance and pain you must *endure* **just to get to** the place of *enduring* the pain of the actual race is incredible!

So why would anyone ever exercise *endurance?* It sounds like no fun at all (it may come down to the definition of "fun" as well). Well, the reason to exercise and experience endurance comes down to "the end goal" is defined.

See, if "fun" is the end goal, endurance is not needed. If, on the other hand, pushing boundaries you never thought possible, or exceeding what you have done before, or inspiring others to pursue a difficult/lofty aim is your *goal*...endurance will be needed.

Nothing worthwhile, grand or lasting, is generally easy. When you pursue goals that are worthwhile and grand it will require hardship, sacrifice and pain. To not allow things to slow or even stop you from the larger goal (Finish Line) you must run with *endurance*...and yes, pain.

QUESTION: With this one and only life you have to live what are your goals? Are they lofty, grand, boundary-breaking, and envelope-pushing? Or are your goals primarily to have "fun" (however that may be defined), to seek ease, to be comfortable and at all costs to avoid pain?

CHALLENGE: Write down a list of goals that are as big as you can imagine today. Toss out all concern for the cost of such goals for the moment and strictly focus on what you would do IF you knew you could not fail. Then begin to pursue them recognizing that you will need to run this race with endurance!

_____

_____

_____

_____

_____

_____

# CLEAR EYES (VISION) VS. CLOUDED EYES (VISION)...

*"The eyes are the window of the soul.*
*If the eyes are full of light the whole body is full of light*
*but if the eyes are dark, the whole body is dark."*
*Luke 11:34*

THIS VERSE STRUCK ME in a strange way one cool day during a training run. I remember that day because it was so cool and sunny. I had on a number of layers, along with gloves, a hat and my sunglasses.

After going a few miles, my body was warmed up and I was sweating. Very slowly, almost imperceptibly I began to notice my sunglasses were fogging up (apparently from the way the heat was being trapped by my hat). The further I went, the more my glasses were covered, and the more difficult it became to see the path in front of me.

I began thinking about how our eyes are the window, the gateway to our very soul and this verse came to mind. Luke 11:34 says *"The eyes are the window of the soul. If the eyes are full of light the whole body is full of light but if the eyes are dark, the whole body is dark."*

When the eyes are full of light, it is very easy to see the path, and its obstacles, in front of us. Those obstacles, by the way, pose so much less danger and can be easily navigated when they are seen far off.

However, when the eyes become dim or clouded, our vision suffers. We have less and less capacity to see and plan for dangers or obstructions ahead. We are forced to slow our pace considerably so as to remain sure-footed and give ourselves more to time to react if there is something in the way.

**QUESTION:** Has anything in your life started to fog your vision? Has something crept in that is creating "blind spots" and increasing the risks of getting you hurt? Are you finding your pace is slowing because it is harder to see dangers?

**CHALLENGE:** Write down any "blind spots" you have; any areas in your life including, people, places or activities that are causing you to not see with the utmost clarity. Decide how to "un-fog" your glasses from these things so as to run the best (and most injury-free) race possible.

_____

_____

_____

_____

_____

_____

_____

_____

_____

MILE

11

_____

_____

_____

_____

_____

_____

_____

_____

_____

_____

_____

_____

_____

_____

_____

_____

# Is **That** Really Necessary?

*"... let us strip off every weight that slows us down..."*
*Hebrews 12:1*

ONE DYNAMIC IN A MARATHON that you don't see in shorter races is the "clothes shedding" factor. Generally speaking, marathons are scheduled during the cool months for the host city. Ideally, a race needs to be around 35-45 degrees at the start. This allows a runner to go many miles without sweating profusely and dehydrating.

Because the start of a race is so cool, most runners wear numerous layers. These layers are meant to be "peeled off" as they get warmer throughout the race. Some folks will wear old shirts and sweats (some wear trash bags) so they can peel that layer off, leave it in the street and not feel guilty.

During a marathon in 2003, I had a unique encounter with this verse (..."let us strip off every weight that slows us down..."). As I was deep into the race, I had thrown away a number of layers I no longer needed to stay warm (a trash bag outer shell, 2 old t-shirts and a pair of cotton gloves). This verse began to ring true in that, I no longer needed those items, and if I had continued to hold onto them, they would just slow me down. Then I saw *them*...

Around mile 20, I looked down and saw a pair of very expensive Nike running gloves I had wanted for a long time. They were just staring up at me from the pavement and begging me to pick them up. As I found myself debating whether or not to pick them up (because I just couldn't live without them) I realized the real meaning of this verse. Why did I *NEED* them at this stage of the race? My hands were warm, I had thrown away my perfectly functional cotton gloves and I was already down to the bare necessities to cross the Finish Line successfully.

Thus, at this late stage of the race I had to make a decision. Do I slow down, bend over (both of which can seriously mess up a runner up at this stage) and pick up something I certainly wanted (desired strongly is a better way of saying it!) but had absolutely no use for in helping me cross the Finish Line OR ignore the temptation, realize these gloves would only be a hindrance and keep moving to the end goal?

I PICKED THOSE SUCKERS UP BY GOSH! DO YOU KNOW HOW MUCH A PAIR OF THOSE NIKE GLOVES COST?!? Just kidding. But boy or boy did I ever want to! Instead of picking them up, I "cast off every weight that slowed me down" (and refused to pick up any new weights) so I could finish what I started!

**QUESTION:** What "weights" are slowing you down right now in your race of life? Have you cast off some weights only to find you've picked others up because you think you "need" them?

**CHALLENGE:** Write down those things that you know you no longer need at this stage of your race (even if they were needed and were valuable at an earlier stage). Decide how you will "lay them down" or "cast them off."

The balancing act is to know when you no longer need something and then having the courage to let them go. And whatever you do, once things are cast off, DO NOT pick up anything unnecessary later because you "can't live without it!"

_____

_____

_____

_____

_____

_____

_____

_____

_____

_____

_____

_____

_____

_____

_____

_____

_____

# GETTING THERE FROM HERE

### *"Let us run the race that is <u>marked out</u> for us"*
### *Hebrews 12:1*

WHAT I FIND INTRIGUING about any long race, especially marathons, is the winding and non-linear direction of the actual race course. For example, the Chicago Marathon starts on the same street it ends. The distance between the Start and Finish Lines is only a matter of a few hundred feet. HOWEVER, the course takes off in the opposite direction of the Finish Line and proceeds to wind its way all over the city.

As I ran along this winding route, I began to ponder this scripture... Here I was, along with 40,000 of my closest friends, trotting along a race course that someone else had marked out for us to run.

Because someone else had decided to make this the route, all the runners would see certain sites and experience unique scenery, otherwise known as "eye candy", while many times running in the exact opposite direction from our final destination!

Sometimes the places your race takes you are exciting and encouraging; sometimes though a race's course will take you to dark and very lonely (maybe even, dangerous) places on your way to the Finish Line.

Regardless though, you are running a course that someone else has laid out for you to run. The course may not make sense and may be filled with strange people, smells and places but nonetheless it is YOUR race, marked out for YOU to run. It should be embraced and run with energy and your best effort.

**QUESTION:** Are you questioning the direction of the life race you are in? Does it seem like you are turned around, running in the opposite direction of where you know you need to go? Are there people and sites you find strange or disconcerting?

**CHALLENGE:** Realize your course, very likely, is not a straight line race and it is a winding, sometimes confusing path that requires faith but eventually leads to the goal you most prize.

Write down all the unique places you have been taken thus far. Consider those people you have encountered, either running along with you or cheering from the sidelines. Write down what you have learned, good and bad, from this course and those folks. Determine to run this race (that someone else has marked out for you) to the best of your ability and trust that the Finish Line is there and is worth it!

_____

_____

_____

_____

_____

_____

MILE

13

# CHEATERS NEVER WIN

*"And athletes cannot win the prize unless they follow the rules."*
*2 Timothy 2:5*

IT WAS FUNNY how this verse struck me one day when I was on a long training run. At first it seems like such a straight forward truth, but it goes pretty deep once you begin to ponder it.

In our culture today, we see cheaters in every area of life, business, government, the media, and sports. Sometimes it seems like you almost have to cheat to win. But consider the word "win." What is the bigger picture, the larger concept, the thing ultimately your race is all about? Is it not to "win" while playing by whatever set of rules you were given?

Yes, of course you can possibly "win" a lot of races, titles, games while breaking the rules undetected but did you really win anything? Furthermore, how long can things go undetected? Let me give you a few names and see where your minds goes as to how much they really "won" in the end:

Lance Armstrong, Ryan Braun, Pete Rose, Sammy Sosa, Roger Clemens, Barry Bonds, The Black Sox, the Michigan Fab 5, Ben Johnson, Reggie Bush, and just for fun...Milli Vanilli.

A saying to internalize is, "People will judge you by the worst thing they know about you."

These are just a quick-hit list of folks who, at one time, won something very substantial. However, they ultimately were found to have broken rules they were to play by, which then led to the (public) stripping of the titles/awards/honors/accolades they once held.

All we really have at the end of the day is our integrity. Fact is, there are always rules governing the races in which we are participating. If we compete honestly, within the rules, we have the satisfaction of knowing where we truly stack up. When we bend, break, or ignore the rules we then compete on a skewed scale and we hold prizes that were not fairly won. When we are found out, we lose the prize AND our integrity! Thus, we must play by the rules!

**QUESTION:** What are the rules surrounding the race(s) you are in? Have you broken them? Have you been tempted to break them to obtain a prize? How would you feel if you were known as a "cheater" or were stripped of your honors because of giving into that temptation?

**CHALLENGE:** Make an out-loud verbal declaration that you will play by the rules and you will guard your integrity above all else. Determine that whatever race(s) you find yourself in you will give your very best BUT WITHIN the framework of the rules.

_____

_____

_____

_____

_____

MILE
14

# WHEN YOU SAY YOU ARE GOING TO DO IT, YOU CAN'T BACK DOWN

*"A city on a hill cannot be easily hidden"*
**Matthew 5:14**

"HEY EVERYBODY, I am going to run the Chicago Marathon in October this year." That statement in 2002 set into motion what has now become over a decade of long distance running.

I did not say, "Hey everybody I am *THINKING* about running *SOME* marathon *SOMETIME.*" If that had been my declaration, I could have hidden behind vagueness and a lack of full commitment. A statement like that also does not cause anyone else to stand up, take notice, or potentially follow to do likewise.

In 2002, when I said "I would run *THE* Chicago Marathon in October", people started to take notice. They also began to watch and check up on how my training was progressing. After running the race, they wanted to know how I did and what it was like. A few people decided they would run along with me the next year.

Just like a "city on a hill cannot be easily hidden", so it is when you decide to do something like run a marathon. Your work ethic, progress, pain, set-backs and successes cannot be hidden because you are an example; you become someone to watch and admire...even imitate.

It was a revelation for me to realize that by declaring I would do that race in 2002, and by subsequently continuing to declare I will do races each year, more and more people have become inspired to run long races as well. What an amazing dynamic to be a "city on a hill."

**QUESTION:** What risk or challenge have you PUBLICLY declared you are going after? What mountains do you want (or need) to climb? What is holding you back from declaring today that you are going to attack that mountain?

**CHALLENGE:** Write down ONE mountain you are going to climb (one risk you are going to take, one challenge you are taking on, one race you will run) this year. Once it is on paper, declare it out loud to yourself...and then to others. It is amazing what will happen when you decide to take a risk and stand out from the crowd (to be a "city on a hill") and commit to DO something!

_____

_____

_____

_____

_____

_____

_____

_____

_____

# BEATING A GIANT

*"Goliath shouted, 'Why do you line up for battle?*
*This day I defy (you)...let us fight each other.'"*
**I Samuel 17:8-11**

OK, IT IS EASY TO SEE a marathon as a "giant" that defies all who dare to challenge it. Marathons are BIG obstacles and they have the power to kill. Just ask the first dude that attempted this distance back at the Battle of Marathon, he died running the distance! A marathon is something to conquer, something to beat.

As I stood at the start of my first marathon, I thought about this verse and the story of David versus Goliath. In this situation, I was like David "lining up for battle" at the start line with this "giant" defying me to try my best to beat it that day.

As I thought about that Bible story and how it was an interesting connection to what I was doing that day, I thought about David and how he won that battle. It was at that moment I thought of a famous 20th Century quote that says, "Start where you are. Use what you have. Do what you can." I realized that is exactly how David approached his battle... and how I was going to approach mine.

If you know the story of David and Goliath, you know that Goliath was a giant standing over nine feet tall who had the best armor and weapons of his day and he was looking to fight a champion from the opposing side. The one who came out to fight him was David, a teenage shepherd who had no armor and only a slingshot for a weapon.

However, David lined up anyway and used what he had. With only a rock and sling, he defeated Goliath AND changed the course of history! What I have found, when facing a giant, you have to *start where you are, use what you have and do what you can*. That is the formula for slaying giants.

When I take someone through the process of completing a long distance race, we just begin wherever they are, at whatever fitness level that are that moment. We use what we have, treadmills, streets, roads, other races. And, we do what we can; run what the training calls for today as best as we can.

There will always be giants in our lives defying us to beat them. It is what we do with that challenge that matters.

**QUESTION:** What "giant" is defying you right now? What is that giant saying you cannot possibly do? If he were to fall, what would your life look like? How would things change if that giant was stood up to, defeated and removed?

**CHALLENGE:** Write down every "giant" you are in a battle with today. Write down exactly what words the giant is using to defy you.

As David did, declare to the giant that HE WILL FALL! Picture (in great detail) what your world will look like after that giant is removed completely. Go forward into battle!

_____

_____

# T-SHIRTS VERSUS FINISHER'S MEDALS

*"I have finished the race...there is a crown for me"*
*2 Timothy 4:7-8*

WHAT ARE THE TANGIBLE EVIDENCES and rewards for signing up for and finishing a marathon? There are the t-shirt and the *Finisher's Medal*. A *Finisher's Medal* is ONLY for those who cross the Finish Line successfully and in the allotted time. If you have completed a marathon (or half marathon) you know these are the trophies sought and prized. These serve as the lasting proof and reward for finishing the race.

But...there is a major difference in the two trophies. Finisher's Medals declare you finished the race where the t-shirt on the other hand merely says you signed up for the race. One is about starting the other is about finishing.

Runners tend to judge races by what the official t-shirts and medals look like. The reason is, those two things end up being the only tangible proof you actually participated in that particular race.

T-shirts are temporary though. However, they serve as good conversation pieces. "Oh you did the 2011 Vegas Marathon? Cool... so did I. What did you think about... T-shirts really only tell someone you signed up to run that race; they do not prove you actually finished that race successfully. Additionally, t-shirts eventually stain, shrink, stretch, get lost or simply get tossed. While they tell a portion of the story, they do not last and will never take the place of the medal you receive for finishing the race.

The medal is designed, crafted and produced by the host of the race to be a permanent trophy/ honor/ reward/ "crown" for the runner to tell the story of what they did, where they did it, and how long it took them to do it. It was intentionally made to be a trophy worth attaining and then holding onto...long after the t-shirt has made its way to Goodwill.

The verse above speaks directly to the idea that *finishing* is more important than just *starting* and because so, finishers will receive something much more valuable than those who merely did enough to get a t-shirt.

QUESTION: What trophies are you most proud of that you have received in your lifetime? Why are you proud? Is it because you did more than just start that endeavor? What "t-shirts" have you settled for rather than doing what it takes to get the "Finisher's Medal?" How does that make you feel?

CHALLENGE: Write down the "t-shirts" (those projects, challenges, races, etc...) you have started but not finished yet. Write down the "Finisher's Medals" you have attained so far on another page. Look at the two lists and consider what it says about you. Begin moving t-shirts to medals!

_____

_____

_____

# DRINK TO YOUR HEALTH

*"But he himself will be refreshed from brooks along the way. He will be victorious."*
*Psalm 110:7*

OK HERE COMES AN OBVIOUS STATEMENT... No matter how tall or short, big or small, strong or weak, in shape or out of shape you are, you cannot live without water. We need it for our very existence. Go without it for any prolonged period of time and bad things start to happen. Go without it for too long during a race and REALLY bad things happen!

The only way to complete a long run or a long race is by taking in water/ fluids/ refreshment. The further you go, the more you sweat and the more fluid you need... and the more frequently you need it.

Someone told me before my first marathon, "Take water and Gatorade every time they offer it. If you wait until you feel thirsty, it is too late...bad things are coming."

Anyone who has found themselves miles (and hours) into a race dealing with dehydration and cramps can attest to this statement. To think that something as small as a cup of water every so often can be the difference between victory and defeat or even, life and death, is pretty amazing!

How many times though, have there been water stations runners ignore because they feel that getting a drink will slow their time down too much? The irony is, by NOT slowing down and taking refreshment when offered, their bodies are pushed too hard and they potentially damage themselves to the point of being forced to slow down or even quit!

The only way to victory in a long race is to take refreshment when it is offered!

**QUESTION:** How many "water stops" or opportunities for refreshment have you ignored because you were just too busy, too focused on the end goal, making too good a time to slow down long enough to receive the refreshment being offered? Are you feeling any effects (yet)?

**CHALLENGE:** Consider what opportunities to slow down and receive refreshment are coming. How will you treat those opportunities? Write them down below and plan to take every one offered because if you wait until you know you need one, it may be too late!

_____

_____

_____

_____

_____

_____

_____

_____

MILE

18

71

MILE
19

# THE FAITH PHENOMENON

*"Faith is believing in what you have not seen."*
*Hebrews 11:1*

ONE DAY ON A TERRIBLY and monotonously long run, this verse hit me in a profound way. I remember thinking, "wonder if people realize that we all live our lives by faith?" It struck me that we all live every single day purely on faith, but we rarely acknowledge it.

This revelation struck me because that day I was running all alone, in a traffic-filled street, on a hot summer day *and* I had not told anyone where I was going.

Ok...so think about that for a second, I was completely living on faith during this run. Faith that I would not be hit by a car, faith that I would not dehydrate, and that I would get back home safely. Oh, and the faith that should something happen to me, complete strangers would take care of me because nobody I knew was aware I was even out running! That was a lot of faith to live on for just a training run. Well, guess what? You are doing it too every second of your day.

Consider the faith it took to merely sit in a chair, you don't really know if it can hold your weight. Consider the faith you use to eat meals at restaurants, you don't know the people cooking in the back and how they prepared your food. Consider driving a car and all the faith you have in the vehicle's performance, your driving ability, other drivers and their cars. Think how much faith it takes for you to even function doing the simplest tasks of life...amazing isn't it?

It stunned me that day that the level of faith one needed to train for, and then actually finish a marathon. Faith such as: your body functioning properly, to not being hit by cars while training, traveling by cars and airplanes going to the race site, consuming fluids during the race you assume will not make you sick and on and on.

This idea that we already have a built in capacity for living by faith is one of the most profound lessons God ever showed me from the long run!

**QUESTION:** Have you ever stopped to think about how much faith you live by every single day? Why do you think that is how we are wired up? How far of a leap is it to think then that God made us that way because trusting His promises requires faith?

**CHALLENGE:** Write down below every way you have exercised faith just in the last 3 hours. Take a blank sheet and write down the faith you used to live in the last week (month, year). Take 15 and sit quietly to consider how much faith you already exercise in the race of life. Write down thoughts as to why you think that is so.

_____

_____

_____

_____

_____

# IN THE END, IT'S YOU RUNNING

*"Therefore, since we are surrounded by such a*
*huge crowd of witnesses..."*
*Hebrews 12:1*

EARLIER IN THE BOOK, this verse was a revelation about the strength we can draw when we hear the multitudes cheering us on while we run. But a few years later this verse hit me in a completely different way.

The second revelation was that while we may be surrounded by thousands of fans encouraging us, in the end it comes down to the fact THEY can't run the race for us...only WE can! Regardless how many come out to be a part of your personal "Curb Crew," you are the one held responsible for doing it.

Interestingly, in our race called life, it works the exact same way. In training for a marathon it is only you who wakes early to log the miles day after day, preparing your body and mind for the approaching race. It is you, who has to make the trip to the city of the race, get up the day of the race, and arrive at the start line, on time, dressed and in the appropriate equipment.

This verse says that since we are surrounded by such a huge crowd witnessing what we are doing, we should run well. The foregone conclusion though is that WE are responsible for being in the race to begin with.

While this observation may seem so obvious, how many times do you and I want the cheers of the crowd without taking the responsibility of preparing and being in the right race to begin with?

QUESTION: Are you taking the responsibility for preparing properly for your race? Are you fully aware that while having a crowd of yelling fans cheering you on, nobody can do this race for you?

CHALLENGE: Write these statements down in the space below:

- *The race is mine alone to run.*
- *No one else can run it.*
- *I take full responsibility to run my race today.*

Now consider writing those statements on cards and placing them in strategic locations you will see throughout the day (bathroom mirror, car, desk, etc...).

_____

_____

_____

_____

_____

_____

_____

_____

MILE
20

79

# RESPECT VERSUS FEAR

*"Do not be afraid!"*
*Exodus 14:13 / Haggai 2:5*

ON THAT CRISP AND CLEAR October day in 2002, I lined up with 40,000 others) to run the Chicago Marathon. It was my first marathon and I had a mix of emotions while waiting for the gun to go off.

On one hand, I was so excited. 18 weeks of training had led up to this moment and I had thought about this moment for years. On the other hand, I was terrified as to what lay ahead over the next few hours. The very first person that attempted this distance at the battle of Marathon actually DIED running this far! And even though I somewhat laughed about that poor guy, I fully understood that this race can kill and there was nothing to say I was going to finish or be alive at the end of that day.

There is something to be said about knowing the difference between having a healthy respect for something or a paralyzing fear of the same thing. While so many of these chapters range from the light-hearted to the introspective, this chapter takes a minute to consider the danger of our race and how to handle it.

A marathon, as with the race of life, has danger in it. Before taking it on, a runner has to seriously consider what can happen. Training and preparation cannot be taken too lightly. In our race of life, we have to realize there is danger and we have to prepare ourselves to the best of our ability, but...

We also MUST conquer that fear, press on and run our race regardless of the danger(s). What I found myself saying is, "Make sure you have respect for the dangers but have no fear!"

QUESTION: What are the dangers of the race you are running that have to be considered and respected? What fears do you have that slow you down or hold you back from going after what you most want? What would your life look like if fear were no longer in the picture?

CHALLENGE: Write down every danger you are facing on a sheet of paper. At the top of the page write, "I respect each one of these but I fear none." Live each day with a healthy and sober respect for the dangers but remove fear from the equation and see what starts to happen!

_____

_____

_____

_____

_____

_____

_____

_____

_____

MILE 21

83

# THIS IS HARD

*"Everyone who competes goes into strict training...."*
*I Corinthians 9:25*

THIS LESSON MAY BE one of the most straightforward but don't write it off without spending some time here.

For me this was a "Duh..." type lesson. I remember writing it down in the journal I was keeping all these insights God was giving me and thinking, "Well of course we know this to be true, so what?" Just because it is straightforward does not diminish the lesson.

What I realized was, to run the upcoming marathon I HAD to go into strict training. I HAD to do things on a schedule that required pain, sacrifice and discipline. All of these things we naturally want to avoid if possible. There was no way I could run this race successfully if I did not make my training strict. My definition of my success for that first race was just crossing the finish line upright!

How often we ignore this simple truth that whatever "race" we are competing in, we must incorporate strict training, practicing, repeating, and working. It is the opposite mindset of those who choose NOT to compete.

By the way here is another obvious concept...if you don't compete, you never win!

**QUESTION:** Are you even competing these days? What "competitions are you in right now? Did you go into "strict training" for them or are you "winging it?"

**CHALLENGE:** Write down specific competitions you have been in. Beside them write (in detail) what the training was like preparing you for them. How did you feel during the training? How did you feel after the competition? What is a future competition coming in your life you know will require strict training? Commit now to it!

---

---

---

---

---

---

---

---

---

---

---

---

MILE 23

# RECEIVING A ROBE AND A CROWN

*"I looked and there before me was a great multitude... from every nation... They were in white robes..."*
*Revelation 7:9*

IN 2002, ON THAT BRIGHT, crisp October as I crossed the finish line of the Chicago Marathon, I saw a vision of Heaven; a *revelation* straight from the book of Revelation actually. The verse came alive in the most unexpected fashion.

Before setting the stage for what happened, let me say that I had always heard (and had an ambivalent belief in) the phrase, "We will receive a robe and crown when we get to Heaven." I also understood Heaven would be a place filled with believers from every tongue, tribe and nation. What I could not get my head around (until the epiphany that day) was, how would we recognize all the different people groups in heaven and how the robe and crown thing factored into all that?

In an instant all that confusion became crystal clear! Here's what I saw:

Crossing the finish line that day, my body and brain were spent. While I was exhausted, the race was finally over and I had beaten it; I could now honestly say I was a marathon runner!

89

The very next thing that happened after crossing the finish line was a group of volunteers began shouting to keep all the runners moving forward. If not encouraged to keep moving, most of would just lay down on any available pavement to rest!

These volunteers were assigned to move you along to another set of volunteers who put a "heat sheet" around your body. The "heat sheet" is a Mylar "robe" that looks like a giant sheet of aluminum foil that serves to keep you warm by trapping body heat. From there, you are instructed to move along to another set of volunteers who places a Finisher's Medal around your neck (your "crown"). After these stops are made, you are then "encouraged" to keep moving on to the food table and Family Reunite area.

After I received my "robe" (Mylar heat sheet) and "crown" (Finisher's Medal), I was shuffling along with hundreds of others when a volunteer yelled out, "Oh if you could only see what I see! You people look beautiful shining in the sun! Congratulations...well done!" It was then I looked back and saw it.

There around me on all sides were people from every nation who were distinct in appearance yet were all wearing their shining robes. The sun bounced off those metal sheets in such a way that it was a blinding white and their "crowning" medals were glimmering.

We had finished the race, received the prize and were being ushered to the *Family Reunite* area. If that was not the most tightly encapsulated vision of Heaven, I don't know what is!

QUESTION: What does Heaven look like to you? Where do you get that image from? Anything confusing about the images you have? At the end of this race called "Life" are you looking forward to receiving your robe and crown and hearing, "Well done?"

CHALLENGE: Take some time in a quiet place and write down what you picture happening at the end of your life's race. Write down how you think you are running and how you want to finish. How do you want that to look?

# GOTTA HAVE SOME, "WANT TO"

*"...like a great athlete eager to run the race"*
**Psalm 19:5**

"WHAT A GREAT DAY to see the city...anyone excited out there?" That was the statement and question that blared over the speakers, which were also cranking Bruce Springsteen's "Born to Run".) literally just minutes before the gun went off for the start of the race. The roar from the crowd's responses was deafening, "Yeeeaaaah"..."whooooo hoooo"..."let's go baby"..."lock and load"..."here we go"..."see you in 4 hours"..."we are outta here"..."I feel the need for speed"..."let's do this thing"..."hasta la vista, baby"..."bring it on!"

There were tens of thousands of runners who had been looking forward to this very moment for months or even years. They were (I was) EAGER to run the race!

Even though we all knew it would not be easy, there would be pain along the way and there was a chance we may not even be able to finish, we still were eager for this race...it's why we were all here at that moment in the first place. The excitement of being in the middle of thousands of eager and truly motivated folks all wanting to overcome the same challenge is something every person should experience at least once in their lifetime! It is inspiring and something you will never forget.

**QUESTION:** What race (challenge, opportunity, mountain, etc...) are you EAGER to start? How many others are standing with you wanting to attack the same course? Knowing full well this race has pain and unforeseen challenges waiting, do you still find yourself EAGER to get underway?

**CHALLENGE:** People want to know what race you are eager to run. They are looking for someone who is excited about taking on a challenge. They find themselves drawn to and inspired by those who express and eagerness to run. Look to be the one who genuinely exudes and expresses that eagerness for the race!

Below write down what race(s) you are eager to run. Why? Once you answer those questions then go verbally tell a minimum of 6 people.

_____

_____

_____

_____

_____

_____

_____

_____

_____

_____

MILE
24

95

# FINISH STRONG

*"I press on to reach the end of the race and receive the heavenly prize for which God, through Christ Jesus, is calling us."*
*Philippians 3:14*

As I THOUGHT ABOUT THE STATEMENT and the action of, "Finishing Strong" two separate lessons from the marathon came to me immediately.

### THE FIRST

Before I ran a marathon, I always heard others who had finished one say, "There are really two races inside the 26.2 miles. The first 20 miles, which anyone can do who has followed the proper training. The second is the last 6.2 miles, which is the great unknown."

What they meant was, the first 20 miles are hard, but if you put in the training the way you should and there are no unforeseen problems (severe weather, lack of water, accidental injury, etc.) anyone can traverse that distance.

The second race is the last 6.2 miles. This distance has to be covered AFTER you have been out there for hours, you have pain in areas you were not planning on (toes, back, shoulders), you are battling cramps and you are mentally fatigued (with your mind under a barrage of complaints from your body)!

Finishing strong or "pressing on to the end of the race" becomes the single most important message you place in your mind. It is the only thought you can have and it is the only thought that will override the "shouts" your physical body screams for the last portion of the race.

## THE SECOND

As you would expect in a race as long as 26.2 miles, you see people at the end who are hurting, slowing, locking up or just plain cannot go on (most of those end up laying in the road in various poses of pain).

Without a single-mindedness of "pressing on to the goal" it is very easy to fall prey to stopping and not finishing. Not finishing is THE worst feeling (just ask anyone who has done it). Without "pressing on to the goal for the prize" (in this case a medal) you may not finish. If you cannot cross the finish line, you will receive no prize (thus, no proof you actually completed this trial). Make no mistake the only way to cross is by "pressing!"

**QUESTION:** What is (are) the goal(s) you started running after to begin with? How close are you to them right now? Do you feel fatigued, slowed, hurt, injured, cramped, miserable, lonely, abused, beat-up, just plain ready to quit? Has this race claimed others who started with you?

**CHALLENGE:** Make an honest assessment about your condition mentally, physically and emotionally right now. How do you "feel?"

Realize this, "Feelings" can lie! Make a decision today that you will have a single-minded determination to "press on" to the goal... the prize...the finish line! Write down in your own handwriting that "Today I am pressing on, pressing through, pressing toward to my finish line by putting one foot in front of the other! And I KNOW that by doing the following things I WILL get there!

# YOUR SHOES
# TELL YOUR STORY

*"Take off your shoes..."*
*Exodus 3:5*

IF YOU TAKE A LOOK at your shoes, they actually tell an amazing story. They tell a story of where you have been... literally. Those treads have traveled roads that were potentially full of excitement and energy or fatigue and pain, amazing companionship or tremendous isolation, dark paths or sun lit roads.

In the verse above, God told Moses to take off his sandals because Moses was at a fork in the road in the "race" of his life. By taking his shoes off here, he could look back and see where he had been while at the same time look forward at the road ahead.

In the same way, I realized there is a need for us to pause and "take our shoes off." When we do, we also can reflect on where we have come from, while preparing for where we are going. Looking at the bottoms of your running shoes is a great way to look backwards and forwards simultaneously to take stock of life.

Flip your shoes over....see anything interesting?

**QUESTION:**

Where have you been over the past few weeks, month or years? What roads have you traveled? What types of challenges were on those roads? What "mile markers" have you passed?

**CHALLENGE:**

Take some time and literally sit down and consider the soles of your shoes and think about where you have been. After you have done this, take a piece of paper and write down where you are headed.

_____

_____

_____

_____

_____

_____

_____

_____

_____

_____

_____

_____

_____

_____

# FAMILY REUNION

*"...and the dead in Christ will rise first. After that, we who are still alive and are left will be caught up together with them in the clouds to meet the Lord in the air. And so we will be with the Lord forever. Therefore encourage each other with these words."*
*I Thessalonians 4:14-18*

ONE OF THE BIGGEST REVELATIONS I received from running these long distance races came at the end of my first marathon in 2002. Let me set the stage...

For years, a marathon had been on my bucket list. I had talked about it and had even looked into training programs should I ever decide to attempt one. Finally in 2002, I was encouraged into running the Chicago Marathon by a friend who was making it his first marathon as well.

All summer we did the prescribed training, and on a crisp day in October, we found ourselves nervously excited at the start line with 40,000 other runners. Bang!...we were off and heading into unchartered waters. Exhilarating, frightening, motivating and nerve-racking all at the same time.

We ran mile after mile, taking in the sights and smells. As time moved on, we noticed that our excitement and good cheer were slowly slipping toward numbness and a desire to see this thing over.

For me that race took four hours and 50 minutes. Soreness, pain and fatigue kept making my emotions waffle between wanting to quit and needing to see that Finish Line. Finally as I came to the sign that said, "Mile 26" I knew there was only .2 miles to go and this giant feat would be accomplished. During the few last minutes of the .2, I started thinking about how great it would be to see the finish line, but there would be something even better to look forward to after it…the Family Reunite area!

This is an area set up for marathons and half marathons where the runners can have a specific place to meet loved ones. These areas are just a short past the finish line.

I knew those who came to support me in this race were going to be there. They had "gone ahead of me" and knew that after running my race, I would join them to be together again.

As I thought about all that, I began to cry. Thinking about how after this life's race is over, in heaven, there is a family reunite area marked off for us to join those who have gone ahead and who are waiting for us.

It was truly a remarkable moment recognizing God used this painful, thrilling, tedious and challenging marathon to teach me a much deeper truth about life's race. The finish line will be great, but the reunion with my family, especially my Heavenly Father will be so much greater!

**QUESTION:** When you consider reuniting with family members who have passed away what do you think about? How exciting will it be to meet those in your family tree who were generations ahead of you? How exciting will it be to cross a finish line and hear from your Heavenly dad (and your biggest fan), "Well done (runner), come on in?"

**CHALLENGE:** Write down the answers to each of the questions asked above and spend the next few minutes, hours, days, weeks or years contemplating them.

MILE
.2

_____

_____

_____

_____

_____

_____

_____

_____

_____

_____

_____

_____

_____

_____

_____

_____

_____

_____

_____

# EPILOGUE

## RECOVERY AND REFLECTION

*"For physical training is of some value, gut godliness has value in all things, holding promise for both the present life and the life to come."*
*1 Timothy 4:8*

After every race there is always a period of time you recover. During that time you generally reflect on all that happened. This section is for that purpose.

Over the course of the last decade, God has shown me deeper insights in His Word during time spent running long distances. This book was an attempt to organize those thoughts and share them with you.

My hope is that this compilation causes you to think about the practicality of God's Word and the ways you can use your everyday life to see much deeper things and to experience God's living Word. Most importantly though, this book was designed to challenge you to think about your life and how you are running the race marked out before you.

While we've talked throughout this book about marathons and training our bodies to run well and compete at the highest level, the apostle Paul says, "physical training" does has SOME value but godliness (walking with God and allowing Him into our daily lives) has value in ALL things (emphasis mine)

As you have worked through these pages, my prayer is that you would see how God wants you to know Him personally and how He wants you to know His promises.

This book is a milestone (pun intended) for taking stock of your life. May it serve as a facilitator for introducing you to the God of Universe (the ultimate "Race Coordinator") in new ways. May it also serve as a catalyst for organizing your thoughts about the "race of your life" and how you can run it more victoriously.

God will teach you if you let Him. I love how He can use anything as a classroom ...even time spent on "The Long Run."

_____

_____

_____

_____

_____

_____

_____

_____

_____

_____

_____

# PERSONAL *LESSONS* LOG

The following section was expressly designed for YOU to capture the lessons you have learned (and are learning)!

The page format is the same that was used to create each chapter (Mile) of this book. These pages will help organize your thoughts into lessons that can be shared with others.

Use these pages to write down the insights you have learned along your race. They may be lessons pertaining to Life, Marriage, Business, Athletics, Relationships, etc. Whatever they may be, write them down.

Once written down, share them with others... AND WITH US.

We encourage you to send your lessons to

## www.lessonsfromthelongrun.com

to be considered for future publications.

MILE
___

TITLE HERE

SCRIPTURE HERE

_____
_____
_____
_____
_____
_____
_____
_____
_____
_____
_____

QUESTION:

_____

_____

_____

_____

_____

_____

_____

_____


CHALLENGE:

_____

_____

_____

_____

_____

_____

_____

_____

MILE
_____

TITLE HERE

SCRIPTURE HERE

_____

_____

_____

_____

_____

_____

_____

_____

_____

_____

_____

QUESTION:

_____

_____

_____

_____

_____

_____

_____

_____

CHALLENGE:

_____

_____

_____

_____

_____

_____

_____

_____

MILE
____

TITLE HERE

SCRIPTURE HERE

_____
_____
_____
_____
_____
_____
_____
_____
_____
_____

QUESTION:

_____

_____

_____

_____

_____

_____

_____

_____

CHALLENGE:

_____

_____

_____

_____

_____

_____

_____

_____

MILE

```
┌─────────────────────────────────────────┐
│                                           │
│              TITLE HERE                   │
│                                           │
│                                           │
│                                           │
└─────────────────────────────────────────┘

┌─────────────────────────────────────────┐
│                                           │
│            SCRIPTURE HERE                 │
│                                           │
│                                           │
│                                           │
└─────────────────────────────────────────┘
```

QUESTION:

_____

_____

_____

_____

_____

_____

_____

_____

CHALLENGE:

_____

_____

_____

_____

_____

_____

_____

_____

MILE
___

┌─────────────────────────────────────┐
│                                       │
│              TITLE HERE               │
│                                       │
│                                       │
└─────────────────────────────────────┘

┌─────────────────────────────────────┐
│                                       │
│            SCRIPTURE HERE             │
│                                       │
│                                       │
└─────────────────────────────────────┘

_____
_____
_____
_____
_____
_____
_____
_____
_____
_____
_____

QUESTION:

_____

_____

_____

_____

_____

_____

_____

CHALLENGE:

_____

_____

_____

_____

_____

_____

_____

MILE ___

TITLE HERE

SCRIPTURE HERE

___
___
___
___
___
___
___
___
___
___
___

QUESTION:

_____

_____

_____

_____

_____

_____

_____

_____

CHALLENGE:

_____

_____

_____

_____

_____

_____

_____

_____

# MORE INFORMATION ABOUT *LESSONS FROM THE LONG RUN*

 Submit lessons from your personal long run at:
*www.lessonsfromthelongrun.com*

 Schedule a *Lessons from the Long Run* LIVE Workshop

 Schedule a book signing in your area

 Schedule Jay McChord to run a race in your area

 Inquire about "Bulk Rate" discounts for large quantities of book purchases

*JAY MCCHORD*
*333 W. VINE ST.*
*SUITE 300*
*LEXINGTON, KY 40507*

**jaymcchord@gmail.com**
**www.lessonsfromthelongrun.com**

# ABOUT THE AUTHOR

 JAY MCCHORD is a nationally recognized and highly requested speaker and author. He is an entrepreneur, politician, artist, husband and father. His high-energy, excitement and desire to encourage people to do more than they thought possible has made him a leader in business, government, education and the non-profit world.

Jay McChord's running resume consists (thus far) of:

- Completed 33 consecutive Bluegrass 10,000's in Lexington, KY (the annual 10K race held in McChord's hometown on July 4th)

- Completed 3 full marathons (Chicago 2002, 2003 and 2007)

- Completed 7 half marathons

- Completed 4 "Bourbon Chase" Races (200 mile team relay race held each year in Kentucky)

- Completed 1 triathlon

- Completed countless 5K's

- Has personally trained dozens of novices and non-runners to complete 5K to full marathon races

CPSIA information can be obtained at www.ICGtesting.com
Printed in the USA
LVOW10s0711181213

365661LV00004B/8/P